COLONIAL PEOPLE

The Printer

CHRISTINE PETERSEN

Marshall Cavendish
Benchmark
New York

This publication represents the opinions and views of the author based on Christine Petersen's personal experience, knowledge,
and research. The information in this book serves as a general guide only. The author and publisher have used their best efforts
in preparing this book and disclaim liability rising directly and indirectly from the use and application of this book.

Other Marshall Cavendish Offices:

Marshall Cavendish International (Asia) Private Limited, 1 New Industrial Road, Singapore 536196 • Marshall Cavendish
International (Thailand) Co Ltd., 253 Asoke, 12th Flr, Sukhumvit 21 Road, Klongtoey Nua, Wattana, Bangkok 10110,
Thailand • Marshall Cavendish (Malaysia) Sdn Bhd, Times Subang, Lot 46, Subang Hi-Tech Industrial Park, Batu Tiga,
40000 Shah Alam, Selangor Darul Ehsan, Malaysia

Marshall Cavendish is a trademark of Times Publishing Limited

All websites were available and accurate when this book was sent to press.

Library of Congress Cataloging-in-Publication Data

Petersen, Christine.
The printer / Christine Petersen
p. cm. — (Colonial people)
Summary: "Explore the life of a colonial printer and his importance to the community, as well as everyday life,
responsibilities, and social practices during that time"—Provided by publisher.
Includes bibliographical references and index.
ISBN 978-0-7614-4802-0
1. Printing—United States—History—17th century—Juvenile literature. 2. Printing—United States—History—
18th century—Juvenile literature. 3. Printers—United States—History—17th century—Juvenile literature.
4. Printers—United States—History—18th century—Juvenile literature. 5. United States—History—
Colonial period, ca 1600–1775—Juvenile literature. I. Title.
Z208.P48 2010
686.20973'09032—dc22
2009044588

Editor: Christine Florie
Publisher: Michelle Bisson
Art Director: Anahid Hamparian
Series Designer: Kay Petronio

Expert Reader: Paul Douglas Newman, Ph.D., Department of History, University of Pittsburgh at Johnstown

Photo research by Marybeth Kavanagh

Cover photo by Collection of the New York Historical Society, USA/The Bridgeman Art Library

The photographs in this book are used by permission and through the courtesy of: *The Image Works*: AAAC/Topham, 4;
Mary Evans Picture Library, 9; The National Archives/HIP,15; *Getty Images*: MPI, 6, 16; *Superstock*, 43;
The Granger Collection: 12, 27, 35; *Art Resource, NY*: The New York Public Library, 17; *The Colonial Williamsburg
Foundation*: 20, 23, 28, 29; *Alamy*: Lyroky, 19; *North Wind Picture Archives*: 37, 40

Printed in Malaysia (T)
1 3 5 6 4 2

CONTENTS

ONE

The First Colonial Printer

In the summer of 1638 a young Englishman named Stephen Daye made a decision that would change his life. Daye heard that a ship would soon leave for the Massachusetts Bay Colony, carrying people who were eager to work and live in the New World. A man was needed to run the printing press. Daye saw this as an exciting opportunity. He and his family boarded the ship *John of London* and set off across the Atlantic Ocean to Boston.

Daye's first job came in January 1639 when the Massachusetts colonial government hired him to print a document called The Oath of a Freeman. Every man who came to live in the Massachusetts Bay Colony had to read and sign this paper.

The first printer arrived in the colonies during the mid–1600s. By the mid–1700s, printers were providing the public with government forms, church sermons, advertisements, and a voice for independence from England.

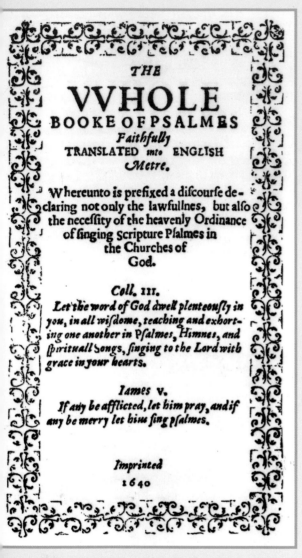

In 1640 the Bay Psalm Book *was the first publication printed in the colonies.*

It was a promise to defend the colony against enemies and to obey all colonial laws. By signing the oath, colonists also agreed never to rebel against the government or the king of England.

Stephen Daye received his most important assignment in 1640. Leaders of the strict Puritan church asked him to print copies of the *Bay Psalm Book*. Puritans considered **psalms** to be the most important teachings in the Bible. The book contained these psalms rewritten as poems, which were easy to sing in church. The *Bay Psalm Book* was the first book written by colonists to be published on a colonial press.

An Information Age

Stephen Daye used a machine called the English common press to print these items. It was not much different from the first European printing press, which was invented in 1440. This printing press had two benefits. First, it used small metal blocks that could be placed together to form words and sentences. These blocks were known as movable type. Each piece of type had a different letter, number, or punctuation mark on it. The printer set up all the pieces of type he needed to make a page of text. When he was done printing, he could take apart the page of type and store the pieces. The second benefit of this press was its speed. The large machine required several workers, but together they could produce many pages of printed material per minute.

Thanks to the printing press, citizens of seventeenth-century Europe lived in an age of information. Just a century earlier most Europeans had been illiterate, or unable to read or write. Only a few thousand books existed, and these were locked away in private libraries or churches. The printing press made books common and more affordable. As a result, reading was no longer a luxury reserved for priests and royalty. Common people began to learn to read, as well. Their lives were often centered around a rural farm or village. Through books, newspapers, and magazines they became familiar with current events in their own country and learned new ideas from around the world.

Colonists brought this same craving for information to the New World. In 1765 John Adams, who would become the second president of the United States, commented, "A Native of America, especially of New England, who cannot read or write is as rare a phenomenon as a comet." Although women, the poor, and people of color had lower rates of **literacy** than white men, colonial people in general were well educated. They valued learning as a tool for success in business, government, and other aspects of life. Some religious colonists also emphasized literacy because it allowed each person to study the Bible independently.

Until the printing trade grew in the colonies, Americans had to find creative ways to satisfy their urge for reading materials. Favorite books were tucked carefully between clothes and other precious belongings for the long journey across the ocean. But these were never enough. Each ship that arrived in a colonial port held boxes of printed material that had been ordered from England. Colonists passed around newspapers and magazines, eager to read news and gossip. They shared poetry and discussed books on history, science, law, politics, and religion.

This system worked, but it was a reminder of the colonists' isolation. It often took months for these materials to arrive by ship from England, and by then the news was woefully outdated. In 1690 William Bird, a colonial farmer from Virginia, complained, "We are here at the end of the World, and Europe may bee turned topsy turvy ere wee can hear a word of it."

Before printing took hold in the colonies, people relied on English publications for their reading material.

Equally frustrating was the lack of communication among colonies. Settlements were often widespread, and the roads were rough. It could take days or weeks to travel between towns. Colonists were eager for newspapers providing current information on colonial events, but many decades would pass before printers would be allowed to fulfill this request.

Permission to Print

Colonists in America were as different as any people could be. There were wealthy businessmen and poor farmers, people with university-level education, and many who were unable to read or write. Just a few decades after colonization, America's population already represented a variety of religious groups. Despite these differences, colonists had one important trait in common. They believed in personal freedom.

The English government feared that these independent colonists might try to rebel. The solution was to prevent colonists from spreading new ideas about religion or government. Beginning in 1662 English laws gave colonial governors control over the printing trade. Governors had permission to stop any printing project that they considered dangerous. One instruction stated that "no person [shall] keep any printing-press for printing, nor ... any book, pamphlet or other matters whatsoever be printed without your especial leave and license first obtained."

Not only did the law restrict the topics that colonial printers could discuss, but it also limited the types of work they could do. English printers were given the best and most profitable projects, including printing the English-language Bible, dictionaries, and encyclopedias. They made all maps and were allowed to publish

The First Colonial Newspaper

Boston printers Benjamin Harris and Richard Pierce took a bold step when they released the first issue of a newspaper called *Publick Occurrences Both Forreign and Domestick* on September 25, 1690. At the time no other newspapers were available to colonists. This one included just the kinds of news that colonists wanted to hear.

Harris wrote an article about smallpox, a deadly disease that had recently struck Boston and other parts of America. In another story he reported that an American-Indian tribe living near Plymouth, Massachusetts, had recently celebrated Thanksgiving in honor of its good harvest. The newspaper would probably have had a different fate if all the stories had been as simple as these. But Harris included gossip about the king of France. He also revealed that the army had killed a number of Mohawk Indians in a prison camp.

Before the day was over, a copy of *Publick Occurrences* made it to the desk of the governor of Massachusetts. The governor ordered Harris and Pierce to shut down the paper immediately. The first issue of *Publick Occurrences* was also the last. It would be almost fifteen years before another printer attempted to publish a newspaper in the American colonies.

Thomas Natt,
CARVER, GILDER,
AND
IMPORTER OF
BRITISH & FRENCH
LOOKING-GLASSES,
ENGRAVINGS, &c.
No. 192,
CHESNUT STREET,
NEAR EIGHTH, PHILADELPHIA.
___

An elegant assortment of Gilt framed Mantel and Pier Glasses.
Mahogany Mantel and Pier Glasses.
Toilet and Swing Glasses.
Orders for Shipping put up as usual.
☞ Picture and Portrait Frames made to any pattern at the shortest notice.

Printing advertisements, such as this, were common projects for the colonial printer.

magazines and newspapers. Colonial printers would gladly have done this work, saving colonists the expense of having the items shipped from England. Instead, most of their time was spent printing government forms, church sermons, advertisements, and business paperwork.

For decades printers were afraid to challenge these laws, knowing that their businesses could be shut down or they could be jailed for printing without a license. This situation would gradually change. As the population of colonists grew, so did their demands for information. Printers began to take risks—releasing newspapers without licenses—and jeopardizing their own safety. In the mid–1770s colonists called for independence from England, and printers became their voices.

TWO

The Printer's Work

Almost every colonial community had its own team of local craftsmen. Colonists could ride from their farms to the nearest village to visit the **blacksmith**, **carpenter**, **miller**, **tanner**, or **wheelwright** whenever necessary. However, they would only find a printer in the largest cities. This location was a practical choice, because it placed the printer close to government offices. Printers spent much of their time producing two types of government documents: forms and laws. Forms were needed to track government spending, to sign up men for the army, and much more. The printer prepared large numbers of these forms and provided them whenever needed. He was also busy any time a new law was passed. Copies of the new law were made and posted in every village for the citizens to read. The printer often sold copies of the laws in his shop, as well.

A very skillful printer might be asked to print currency, or paper money. The printer had to be tricky when designing currency so that it would be difficult to **counterfeit**. He sometimes included special words or pictures that were hard to copy. Colored threads or minerals could also be added to the ink or paper.

Lottery tickets were printed on large sheets and then cut apart. The lottery was an exciting game. Citizens paid a small amount for each ticket. The winner in each game received a prize of cash, land, slaves, or goods. But the real winner was the government. The lottery was its clever way of raising money to pay for improvements in the city or colony.

In between government jobs, printers did a wide variety of projects for their neighbors. They printed sermons to be handed out on Sunday at local churches. Businesspeople sometimes hired them to make **broadsheets**. These were large sheets of paper printed on one or both sides. They often served as advertisements for a product or service and might include pictures as well as text. Local schools always needed primers and hornbooks. Primers were small books used to teach reading, while hornbooks were single sheets of paper that contained individual lessons. Each hornbook sheet clipped onto a small wooden frame with a handle for the student to hold.

One of the printer's most popular items was a yearly almanac. This paperback book contained information that was useful to colonists throughout the year. It included tables of high and low tides to assist sailors, and advice to farmers about when to plant and harvest crops. The almanac also listed interesting events such as fairs and court sessions as well as a schedule of postal deliveries for the year. Colonial women referred to the almanac for new recipes. Travelers used the tables showing distances between inns. And the almanac was a favorite source of entertaining stories, poems, and jokes that could be shared by the whole family.

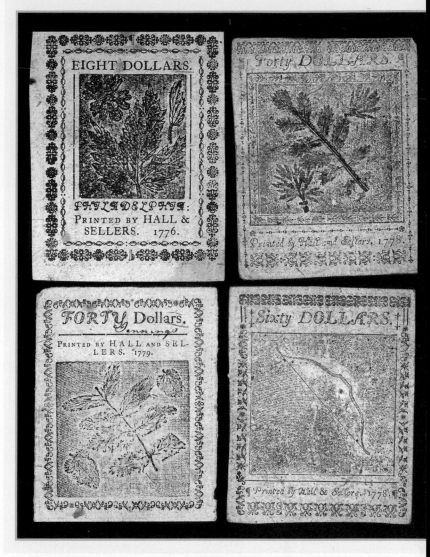

Colonial currency was printed with fine details so it could not be illegally copied.

V. **MAY** Hath 31 Days. 1775.

Who never from the field of battle flies,
But for his children and his country dies,
Ne'er shall his glory fade, or cease his fame
Tho' laid in dust, immortal is his name.
But if the sable hand of death he shun,
Returning victor, with his glory won;

First Quart. 7 Day, 2 Aftern. | Last Quart. 21 Day, 9 Aftern.
Full Moon, 15 Day, 4 Morn. | New Moon, 29 Day, 4 Morn.

[Ames, 1775.]   B

Almanacs were printed every year in the colonies. They contained useful information for the colonists. This page features the month of May 1775.

Making a Living

When necessary, the printer found creative ways to increase his income. It was not unusual for him to use a corner of the print shop as a stationery stand. He stocked popular items such as paper, pens, pencils, and ink. The printer could also sell books. Some of these were printed in his shop; others were imported from England.

It also made sense for the printer to become the postmaster for the region. The postmaster was hired by the government to receive and organize all the mail. Colonists who lived in town came to the print shop to collect their letters. As postmaster, the printer supervised postriders who delivered mail by horseback to distant cities, villages, and farms. However, colonists had to be patient. Roads were rough and did not reach into every part of the colonies. Delivery depended on many factors—especially the availability of riders and fresh horses. Even in good weather it might take four weeks for a letter to cross the 500 miles between Boston, Massachusetts, and Williamsburg, in Virginia Colony.

A postmaster hands mail for delivery to the postrider in 1775 Philadelphia.

THREE

The High Cost of Printing

By colonial standards printing was a very expensive trade. The printer was rarely able to afford all the equipment necessary to start his own shop. More often a wealthier colonist purchased the large printing press, a set of movable type, and a stock of paper and ink. For many decades these items had to be shipped from England, adding to their expense. Once the press was set up, some owners left all the work to the printer and his assistants. Others were in the shop every day, managing the business and controlling the money. An owner might even edit or write stories for a newspaper. Whatever role the owner played, it was the printer's experience and skill that made the business really successful.

Type and Press

A print shop needed at least one press to begin printing. The English common press was large and bulky, filling an entire corner of the shop from floor to ceiling. Some shops had as many as three presses. The additional equipment allowed the owner and printer to take on more projects. However, it also required them to hire more help, for it took at least two men to run each press.

The printer needed one or more sets of movable type. A single set of type contained many blocks for each letter, in both capitals

This tray shows the many blocks of movable type used by the printer.

This print shop in the re-created town of Colonial Williamsburg, Virginia, features printers working on a document.

and lowercase. There were extra copies for letters such as *e*, which are used more frequently than other letters in the English language. The total number of blocks in a set was enough to make hundreds of words.

Eleven type styles were available to printers in the 1600s. By 1770 printers could choose from seventeen different types. Each produced print with a different size and appearance: large or small, simple or ornate. The printer could get by with just one set, though the metal pieces tended to wear down from frequent use. Ideally, the shop had several sets of type. This allowed the printer to be more creative when designing the layout of the documents.

Paper and Ink

The printer also used large quantities of ink and paper. Making ink involved a smelly procedure in which flaxseed (also known as linseed) oil was slowly boiled with rosin, a type of hardened pine sap. When this sticky mixture cooled, **soot** was added. Called lampblack, this soot gave ink its black color.

Paper was even more difficult to make. Colonial-era paper was made from cloth rather than wood, as it is today. The printer collected worn-out clothing from neighbors and family until he had a large supply. The cloth was torn into strips and beaten with

Women's Work

In 1685 William Nuthead became the first printer in the colony of Maryland. Assisted by his wife, Dinah, Nuthead did steady business and specialized in printing business forms. When he died unexpectedly ten years later, Dinah was left with no source of income to support their family.

Dinah Nuthead was a strong woman, and she decided to keep the print shop open. To become a printer, Dinah had to get a license from Maryland's colonial government. This was not an easy step for anyone, let alone a woman. Colonial America was a traditional society. A woman might help her husband in his business, but she almost never ran one by herself. No colonial woman had ever been given a printing license, yet Dinah convinced the Maryland government that she was up to the job. She promised to faithfully follow all the printing laws and paid a massive fee of one hundred English pounds to prove her commitment.

Dinah had one last problem to overcome. She was illiterate, or unable to read or write. So she hired a young printer to set up the type before printing. Dinah was an excellent businesswoman and soon became a trusted printer for the Maryland government.

A craftsman collects pulp that will be made into paper in Colonial Williamsburg, Virginia.

hammers to reduce the fabric to a pulpy ball. This ball was placed in a huge vat with water. The wet pulp was scooped out using a wire strainer. The printer spread the pulp evenly across a rectangular wooden frame. Wire mesh on the bottom of the frame allowed water to flow out as the printer pressed on the pulp. When dry, the sheets were usually thick and yellowish.

The printer was commonly trained to make these essential materials. However, he rarely had the time or space necessary to do this painstaking work. The result was never satisfying anyway: his homemade products always seemed to be rough and ugly. The printer preferred the high-quality ink and paper he could buy from England. However, he had to pay taxes on every order, making the products much more expensive.

In 1690 the first paper mill was built near Philadelphia. The mill had a large wheel that was placed in a rushing stream. The wheel's spinning motion turned a set of hammers, which pounded the cloth into pulp. A print shop in Boston finally began to produce high-quality ink in the mid–1700s. Other printers ordered this ink in large amounts and were happy to wait for its arrival, even if the mail delivery took weeks or months.

Access to locally made paper and ink reduced the printer's effort and expense. However, a century after the arrival of Stephen Daye, only about fifty print shops could be found in all of the thirteen colonies. The enforcement of harsh English laws still made printing a risky business that most people were unwilling to try.

FOUR

Running the Press

Any colonist with money could buy a small printing press. Counterfeiters sometimes did this, secretly using the press to forge paper currency. However, a legal print shop was a large operation that required many people in order for it to run smoothly. Printers took pride in doing excellent work and closely supervised everyone in their shops—from slaves to the most skilled members of their staff.

The Printer's Apprentice

Colonial boys rarely chose their own jobs. Those who did not become farmers, and who could not afford college, had to learn a trade. This required completing an apprenticeship. The apprenticeship was a training period during which a boy lived and worked with a master craftsman. The choices of jobs were often limited, because each community had only a certain number of craftsmen.

Before beginning to work, the boy had to sign an **indenture** with his new master. This contract outlined the terms of the apprenticeship. The boy agreed to work hard and always obey the master. The master promised to teach him the "art and mystery" of his trade. He also provided the boy with food, clothing, and shelter over the years.

An **apprentice** was little more than a servant. He often worked from sunup to sunset, and Sunday was his only day off. The master could beat the apprentice if he misbehaved, and the boy was severely punished if he tried to run away. But if he worked hard, the apprentice could earn his master's trust—and a few privileges, as well. When his indenture was complete, the young man was well trained and ready to make his way in the world.

At first the apprentice was trusted only with jobs so simple that a child might have done them. The boy swept paper from the floor, and he scrubbed ink from the press until his clothes and skin were covered in dark smudges. He ran errands all over town. A hardworking apprentice was gradually entrusted with more responsibility. He practiced laying out the type inside wooden trays called **galleys** to make pages of text. He learned to make ink, run the press, and fold the printed pages. If the printer had his own newspaper, a clever apprentice might even be given the opportunity to write some text. During the evenings, the master taught his apprentice reading, writing, and arithmetic. A printer was expected to be well educated and needed these skills to run his business.

Over a period of about seven years the apprentice became familiar with the rhythms of the print shop and the operation of all its equipment. The printer rewarded him with a promotion to **journeyman**. The journeyman could work as a paid employee in the shop or move elsewhere to work for another printer. A journeyman printer's income was about four times greater than that of an average laborer in colonial America.

A printer's apprentice gathers type that will be laid out in galleys to make a page of text.

Letters and Words

The journeyman spent years continuing to fine-tune his skills in the printing trade. Often he was hired as a **compositor**. In this job he laid out the tiny blocks of movable type to form words and sentences for printing. The compositor was paid based on how much type he could set up in a day—so he learned to be quick. All of the type was stored in boxes, with each letter, number, or other piece in its own compartment. The compositor memorized the location of each piece so he could grab the type without looking.

Rows of type were laid out inside long, narrow trays called composing sticks. A separate composing stick held each line of text.

This printer lays out type on a composing stick.

Galleys are prepared for the printing press.

Handling the tiny pieces of type was tricky, but it was not the hardest part of the job. The compositor had to set up all of the text backward. This way when the paper was pressed into the type, a mirror image that read correctly would be produced.

All of the composing sticks for a single page were lined up to form columns inside a galley. The compositor's next step was to check the accuracy of his work. He did not want to run the large press to make one copy. Instead, the compositor made a copy by hand. He spread ink all over the galley and laid a piece of paper on top. Next he pressed a block of wood against the surface of the paper. The inked paper was sandwiched between the wood and type, producing an imprint.

Make a Letter Press

Movable type made printing faster, but printing was done long before this technology was invented. A common technique was called wood-block printing. This type of printing began in China almost two thousand years ago. The printer cut and smoothed a flat slice of wood. He used delicate tools to carve the wood until words or pictures stood out on the surface. Ink was spread over the block, and paper or fabric was placed on top. The image could be transferred onto the paper in two ways: by rubbing the surface of the paper with a hard object or by pressing something heavy onto it.

You can make a simple version of this type of printing press by carving letters into slices of potato. This activity involves the use of a knife, so be sure to work with an adult.

You Will Need

- newspaper
- sweet potatoes or baking potatoes
- a utility knife
- a ballpoint pen (black)
- a ruler
- a small bowl or plastic lid
- acrylic paint (any color you like)
- a sponge
- white paper or parchment paper

Instructions

1. Find a good work space with a flat table. Cover the table with newspaper.

2. Carefully cut the potatoes in half with the utility knife.

3. Using the pen, draw a letter on the cut surface of one piece of potato. Remember that you need to make the letter backward! That way when you print it, the image will be reversed.

4. Place the ruler on the outside skin of the potato. Measure down about 1/4 inch below the cut surface of the potato. Mark a dot at this spot. Make several more dots around the edge of the potato. Connect them to make a line.

5. Use the utility knife to carefully cut away the potato above the line. Cut around the outline of your letter. The letter will be raised above the rest of the potato like the image on a rubber stamp.

6. Place a fresh piece of newspaper on the table.

7. Pour a small amount of acrylic paint into a bowl or plastic lid.

8. Dip the sponge into the paint. It does not need to be soaked.

9. Wipe the sponge across the surface of the letter on your potato. Keep paint off the rest of the potato.

10. Press the potato onto the paper. Do not push too hard—the potato may slip or break. Make sure that the entire letter touches the paper for several seconds.

(continued)

11. Lift the potato straight off the surface of the paper. Your letter should appear clearly on the paper.

12. Allow the paint to dry. (Acrylic paints usually dry within a few minutes.)

13. Practice making better impressions of the letter until you can do it perfectly and then make more letters with the additional pieces of potato. You can spell out messages and even make signs with your potato press.

When the ink dried, the compositor and printer read this page carefully for errors. To correct mistakes, the compositor removed or replaced individual pieces of type. The galley was checked repeatedly until it was perfect. In total, it often took the compositor twenty-five hours to prepare a galley for one page of a newspaper. The process might be quicker when laying out broadsheets or books, which often used larger type or contained drawings.

Galleys were not held together firmly enough to withstand the pressure of a printing press. Before printing they were set into a sturdier wooden frame called a chase and bound tightly into place. The printer could arrange two galley pages side by side in the chase and print them together on a large sheet of paper.

After the paper dried, he printed different text on the opposite side. When the sheet was folded, it formed a tidy pamphlet or a series of pages that fit together as a book or newspaper.

You Can't Judge a Book by Its Cover

The colonial printer was sometimes hired to print books. Customers might even buy these books in his shop. However, one thing was missing from the book: a cover. The bookbinder was a specialized craftsman who bound and covered books.

The book was printed in sections called signatures, which were made from numerous pages folded together according to page number. The bookbinder started by sewing each signature to a piece of fabric. The signatures were then stacked and gently tapped with a hammer to align them evenly. A knife was used to trim the paper, creating smooth edges. The final touch was a cover. Hard covers were glued onto the front and back of the book to protect the pages between them. Depending on their budget, customers might choose inexpensive cardboard or fabric stretched over wood for the cover. They could also have a cover specially made from ornately dyed and decorated leather.

Power of the Pressmen

Unlike compositors, pressmen were not trained printers. They were usually common laborers hired to work in the print shop. Working the press was a backbreaking job, requiring endurance and strength. These qualities earned the pressmen respect and appreciation among the print shop employees.

Two pressmen always worked together and relied on skill and speed to get the job done. They began by placing the chase on the table of the printing press. One man's job was to coat the surface of the chase with ink. This messy task was accomplished with a simple tool that resembled a handheld dust mop. It consisted of a ball of cloth bound in leather and mounted on a stick. The pressman dipped the ball in ink and pounded it on the chase. Then he quickly ran a smooth-edged knife over the entire surface to ensure that ink coated every part of the text. At the same time, the second worker dipped a piece of paper in water and attached it to a wooden box that hung above the table.

As soon as the chase was inked, the other man pulled a handle on the side of the press. This caused the box to drop, pressing the paper against the chase. The second pressman held the handle down for fifteen seconds, using all of his strength to make sure that the image was printed clearly. Then he lifted the lever, and the paper was removed carefully to prevent smearing. A well-coordinated press team could run off 250 pages on the press in an hour. After the paper had hung to dry for a day, the opposite side could be printed if necessary.

Finished materials were sent to the papermen. These workers sorted the pages and put them together in the correct order, folded them, and trimmed the edges to make them look tidy. The job was now complete.

After the chase is inked, the printer pulls a handle causing the box to drop, pressing the paper to the chase.

FIVE

Printing a Revolution

The eighteenth century was a time of significant change in the American colonies. The population grew rapidly, increasing from 280,000 in the year 1700 to more than 2.5 million by 1770. The makeup of the colonies changed, as well. Immigrants began to flood in from European nations beyond England, including Scotland, Ireland, France, Holland, and Germany. A steady stream of people from Africa and the West Indies, who were brought to the colonies as slaves, added another level to this diversity. These slaves represented almost 18 percent of the colonial population, with some regions having larger numbers of slaves than others. Colonists may have come to the New World seeking religious freedom or a way to get rich quickly. Now they imagined America as an independent nation, free of English taxes and trade regulations, and governed by its own citizens.

Farming remained the most important occupation in the colonies. But more and more colonists were drawn to city life. Cities offered a variety of jobs and a rich social life. Colonists gathered in taverns, coffeehouses, and shops. They met in church meetinghouses and at exclusive clubs. Universities were established in some of these towns, and those men who could afford it traveled to broaden their understanding of the world. However simple or powerful their role was in society, colonists eagerly exchanged ideas about politics, trades, and religion.

Changing Times

As these ideas swirled around him, the printer was forced to make a decision. He could no longer ignore the call for news and information. America's first real newspaper, *The Boston News-Letter*, was printed in 1704. It was only a single sheet

The first American newspaper, The Boston News-Letter, *was printed in 1704.*

of paper. Much of the space was taken up with announcements and public notices. However, two columns of newsprint filled each side of the *News-Letter*, printed in the tiniest type size. The printer crammed a wealth of information about events in Boston, the colonies, and the world into this small space. *The Boston News-Letter*—and its printer—received some criticism but remained in print for fifteen years. Other printers were encouraged to take a similar risk. By 1740 a dozen newspapers were available to readers in Boston, Philadelphia, New York, Virginia, and elsewhere.

Every printer was cautious when he first began to print a newspaper. He knew that the government was watching and so was careful not to anger anyone in power. One solution was to remain objective. He simply printed the news, leaving his own opinion out of the story. He might even print both sides of an argument in the newspaper. This way, colonists could form their own opinions.

As the number of newspapers grew, printers felt more confident about printing their opinions on political and social problems. This sometimes led to a conflict between newspapers or drew criticism from readers. One of the earliest printed quarrels took place in 1721. That year a dreaded disease called smallpox struck Boston, taking hundreds of lives. Some physicians encouraged the use of a new medical treatment called inoculation, which they believed could prevent the spread of smallpox. The procedure involved scratching the skin and applying a small amount of the virus in the wound. The patient became slightly ill but recovered quickly and was immune to the disease afterward. Benjamin Franklin's family paper, the *New England Courant*, published articles criticizing inoculation. One article called the treatment a "desperate remedy," and opponents claimed that inoculation would spread the disease. Several other colonial papers stood firmly in support of the treatment. They printed information about the numbers of people who had survived and remained healthy afterward. The back-and-forth arguments became angry and went on for months. In the end inoculation was accepted and became commonplace for the treatment of smallpox and many other contagious diseases.

Government officials kept a watchful eye on printers and publishers in case they became too bold. Their fears were realized in 1734 when New York newspapers began to criticize Governor William Cosby. Readers learned that he had unfairly fired a judge and attempted to block certain colonists from voting. Governor Cosby was determined to stop the stories, but their authors were unknown. Instead, he obtained an arrest warrant for the newspaper's printer, John Peter Zenger.

Andrew Hamilton defends printer John Peter Zenger, establishing freedom of the press.

Zenger was charged with seditious libel—speaking words with the goal of starting a rebellion. Zenger's attorney, Andrew Hamilton, understood that libel could be punished even if the words were true. When his client came to trial in August 1735, Hamilton attacked this idea. He said that colonists should have the right to prevent government abuses "by speaking and writing truth." After considering the case, the jury came back with a verdict of "not guilty." The Zenger trial made it clear that colonists supported freedom of the press.

Printers did not always find it easy to engage in this kind of debate. But it became hard to avoid. Many American colonists were increasingly restless and full of frustrations. They felt taken advantage of by the English government and king. The English government tightened rules controlling trade in the colonies and added heavy taxes to goods purchased or sold by colonists. Worse yet, all of these laws and taxes were approved without any input from colonial leaders.

Printers became especially active in politics after the passage of the Stamp Act in 1765. This law would have required colonists to pay a tax on every item made of paper. Not only were mailing stamps taxed, but also newspapers, books, and everyday documents. A fee was added to each piece of legal paperwork, including marriage licenses, the documents used when selling land, indentures for apprenticeship, and more.

Benjamin Franklin might have been wrong about inoculation, but he came to understand that printers and other colonists could not afford the Stamp Act. Franklin argued against the tax before members of the English government while American protesters burned stamped paper in the streets and harassed tax officials. The law was cancelled, but the damage had been done. Some colonists were eager to gain independence from English rule, and many printers supported their cause. Their printing presses became more than machines to copy words. They were tools for spreading the idea of revolution.

The Most Famous Printer

Benjamin Franklin is known as one of America's great inventors and patriots. He might also be called the nation's most famous printer. Franklin grew up in Boston in the early years of the eighteenth century. At the age of twelve he was apprenticed at the print shop owned by his older brother, James. Franklin was a quick learner and became familiar with every part of the business. He settled in Philadelphia to finish his training.

In 1728, the year he turned twenty-two, Franklin opened a small print shop. Eventually he would become the most successful printer in the colonies, with three large print shops and his own newspaper. Although there were other papers available in the city, his newspaper, *The Pennsylvania Gazette*, became a favorite among readers.

Benjamin Franklin believed in the power of the press to inform and excite people. He worked hard to gather stories on many different topics and made sure that the articles were interesting and accurate. Franklin often published his own opinions or letters commenting on society or the government. His goal was to get people talking about a particular issue. He always used an **alias** when writing such material, knowing that his readers or the government might be angered by the idea. Ben Franklin strove to make his newspaper accessible to everyone. Because many colonists were illiterate, Ben provided cartoons and drawings that explained the news in pictures.

Glossary

alias	a false name
apprentice	a person who trains to learn a new skill or job by working with an expert
blacksmith	a craftsman who shapes iron and steel
broadsheet	a large printed document used as a handout, often advertising a product or service
carpenter	a craftsman who builds or repairs wooden objects
compositor	a printer whose job is to arrange movable type into pages of text
counterfeit	to copy money or other materials
galley	a wooden tray containing strips of movable type set up for printing
indenture	a contract requiring a person to serve an employer for some period of years as a worker or apprentice
journeyman	a craftsman who has completed an apprenticeship
miller	a person who grinds grain into flour
psalm	a sacred song or poem originally from the Bible
literacy	the ability to read and write well enough to communicate
tanner	a worker who treats animal hides to make leather
soot	a powdery, black substance left when coal or wood is burned
wheelwright	a craftsman who makes or repairs wheels

Find Out More

BOOKS

Collard, Sneed B. *Benjamin Franklin: The Man Who Could Do Just about Anything.* New York: Marshall Cavendish Benchmark, 2007.

Kalman, Bobbie. *A Visual Dictionary of a Colonial Community.* New York: Crabtree Publishing Company, 2008.

Winter, Kay, and Larry Day. *Colonial Voices: Hear Them Speak.* New York: Dutton Children's Books, 2008.

WEBSITES

Benjamin Franklin and His Printing Press

http://sln.fi.edu/franklin/printer/printer.html

Learn more about Ben Franklin's career as a printer and writer.

Colonial Printer and Binder

www.history.org/Almanack/life/trades/tradepri.cfm

The Colonial Williamsburg website offers a closer look at the work of a printer.

Colonial Williamsburg Kids' Zone

www.history.org/kids/

Tour the colonial capital of Virginia and meet some of its important residents. There are games and activities, and many resources about colonial life and history.

Index

About the Author

Christine Petersen has written more than three dozen books and several magazine articles for a variety of audiences, from emerging readers to adults. Her subjects include science, nature, and social studies. When she's not writing, Petersen and her young son enjoy exploring the natural areas near their home in Minneapolis, Minnesota. Petersen is a member of the Society of Children's Book Writers and Illustrators.